Flocks of Words

Flocks of Words

Kate Innes

*For Annemarie
with all best wishes*

Kate Innes

**Mindforest
Press**

Flocks of Words

Kate Innes

ISBN: 978-0-9934837-3-8

Published in 2017 by Mindforest Press
www.kateinneswriter.com

Printed in Great Britain by:
The Russell Press Ltd.

Cover Artwork: 'Call of the Birds' from the Apocalypse B.L. MS. Roy. 19 B.xv, f.37v – Public Domain image
Cover Design by macreative.co.uk

For

Dana John Graham Osborn

Contents

Flocks of Words   9
Walking the Hills   10
Mind Forest   12
Dendrochronology   13
Winter River   14
The Morning Path   16
Late Light   17
Clay   18
Breton House   20
Snowfall   22
Constellation   23
Three Fires – Solstice Song   24
Autumn Findings   26
Red Stag   28
The Other Land   29
Creation Myth   30
White Horse   32
Magpie Song   34
If you hope to find   35
Reindeer Hunt   37
Virgin and Child   38
Infante Felipe Próspero   39
The Mother Speaks   40
Where it may lead   42
Fishing   43
Quarried   44
A Girl at Plage d'Erromardie   46
Waters   47
Leverets   49
Spring Lamb   50
Sleeping Dogs   51
Chameleon   52
Words of the Naturalist   53
Redbreast   54
Stained Glass Sequence   56
Acknowledgements   67

(i)

Mind Forest

Flocks of Words

Imagine a country where words were like birds
and flew away surreptitiously,
migrating for whole seasons, leaving one bereft
of noun, verb and preposition.

It begins in autumn when scientific names fly free.
Binomial pairs depart, fast and wild,
and taxonomic flocks coalesce
into Greek, their deltas pointing far away.

Soon all common things become obscure
like the unseen stars at the edge of space,
and in the thrumming fields and naked gardens,
it is like Eden before Adam spoke.

Imagine visiting that land in the spring
and watching the words return,
grown fat with the food of foreign meanings,
their syllables strange to the tongue.

I could enjoy a season unnamed and free,
surrendered to instinct or god's purpose.
But then I'd watch for its approach on tired wings,
and feel the weight of it alighting on my breast,
and put it on, like fresh plumage or a newly laundered
dress.

Walking the Hills

*"I distinctly recollect the desire I had of being able to know
something about every pebble in front of the hall door."
Charles Darwin*

On this illusion of solidity
continents have crunched their bones,
inner earth has spilt its heat.
The scar is this gravelled spine of hills,
sweetly covered in mossy, heathered coats.

The Lawley rises to a ridge,
that points to future sky.
Caradoc follows, glancing back.
From here we are travelling north
by a fingernail's width each year,
the millennia trailing after us,
scattering rocks across the world.
The ground beneath our feet
has flowed and frozen and thawed
into lichen puffs and flowered grass.

We continue on our path,
finding the pebbles, gazing at their souls,
as if they were the events of our lives,
as if they were maps for us to follow.
They tell us deserts have turned to stone,
been built and fallen into ruin.
Bogs have squeezed and sucked to coal.
Rivers have redrawn the world
sending out their ribbons of mud,
their rippled sediment.

Everywhere trace prints
and carapace remain –
space-gathered
animate elements
pressed in layered pages.

We walk this earth
from which we came,
every pebble known
and unknown,·
we walk and return –
becoming dust,
making stone.

Mind Forest

I slip through shadows
into tangled light,
finding the winding way of the happily lost,
past small neat holes,
homes for secrets hung with moss,
and the muscular yew
bowed into sanctuaries
for nests and hoards.

On the ground, the merest touch
remains of pads and claws,
but scents are stronger,
traces of past journeys
marked with musk.
And other remnants
of its darker dreams:
feather ghosts and scat.

There are many paths
and I will not leave
until they have let me in
to crawl along their roots
digging with my fingernails
for tiny jawbones, shrew skeletons,
teeth, talons, beaks.

They are all here under the slow drop
of digested leaf,
the incremental humus
that buries my thoughts
and hatches the green bud
and the blind worm.

Dendrochronology

From this distance it could be dead –
the trunk crazed, limbs drunk,
sparsely haired, clutching
at its scattered leaves.

Inside the hollow oak, the years'
marbled, directionless lines
stretch, contract – are petrified.
Deluge and drought
and the many steady seasons become
a geological section in miniature.

When I put my hands on the inner rings,
I feel a force – not history, but experience.
How long since it was acorn?
How long till I am oak?

Winter River

This winter river is unadorned. No birds or casting lines.
The fishermen are all inside, asleep in chairs,
and I am here, below a shapeless sky.

The river is empty and full, flowing and still,
like sunlight that shows no matter or motion.

I walk with this water, measuring my stride
against its quicksilver, inky flow.
Cold slides through the whips of bare willow,
while each step moulds the sucking clay.

A dog, barking from the sloping lawn, insists I stay
on this untidy bank. And I shall.
For here is the bend where the tree grows,
still hung with yellow apples,
bright and small, un-withered and inedible.

And soon I will see the hoof prints and follow them
along this old gallop field,
held in the river's curved arms,
with all those who waited to cross long ago,
watching the shallow boats
and cursing the churned-up earth that made them slip.

When hooves outnumbered shoes,
and the cattle waited for the boy
who drove them across the ford with his stick.

Before the drone of the road.
In the time when the slice of oars and poles
split the shining water down to twisting roots,
and the river vein healed itself with eddies,
with swimming sky,
with swans and spawn.
With rain.

The Morning Path

Early – almost cloudless sky, low moon.
Young leaves sprinkled with blossom
block the lower view, but it is no matter.
Frost and weed have cracked the lane
and I must watch my feet – the path is steep.

At the first gate, flocculent sheep
gather like colonies in a petri dish.
Behind the second, a field of rape,
engineered, sprayed and fed
in rows of identical nodding heads.

Hill top at last, and the third gate
where I lean and look.

On this lunar morning all the creases
of this familiar body belong to me –
folds of spawning streams, wisps of bees,
the hollows made by muscular hills
and the downy skin of mown grass.

All the compass points are mine –
south, southeast, the bristled beard
on Wenlock Edge is growing soft,
while brown trees on the eastern ridge
go barefoot on mosaics of anemones.
To the north, the Wrekin sleeps
under a tangled sheet.

And in my west, the long slope of field,
where a white buck came ghostly
up the furrows in winter air,
now holds the trembling throat of the lark,
falling – rising.

Late Light

It has rained all day
     and the air is wet wood smoke

but just now – at eight
     the sun has caught us – heedless

it has emerged from its bed of cloud
     only to show us where we live

a world moulded and brushed
     with subtle fleeting fingers

each field – a plain of perfect blades
     each brick – a radiant coal

at last – we breathe it in
     the place we have hidden from all day

a deep sky gapes to swallow
     the delicacy of light into dark blue

but the sun throws out its sly and lustrous net
     and we cannot stop seeing

we live here – we blink
     and then the sun sinks

hours ago this is how it sanctified the barley
     and grass across all the Russian steppes

Clay

Take it in your hands –
this – which is just
dust and water –
a wedge, a lump
weighing heavy in the palm.

Simple gravity
made of the smallest
bits of stone
and a milled mulch
of long dead leaves –

beings mixed and blended
by the water's flow
and the slow grind of seasons.

Push in your thumb, and press
as if you held the hand
of a small child
or an old man –
a thing about to change.

There it will coil or flatten
at your will, score, smooth
or spin into symmetry.

The finger touch of slip
across a cracking edge
will leave your mark
in swirls and whorls –
and it will mark you in return –
puckering you
with its dusty skin.

Add carbon's heat –
a fix of fire –
and it will endure
from the ingenious past
to the curious future.

It is a vessel we fill –
a blank wet slate
on which we scratch
our human state.

Breton House
For Neville Carlton

The old English painter has come
with his hat, brushes, tubes and stool.
Curious, three hens approach
and cock their heads
but they must wait their turn.
For, while the light falls to the west,
the house is purple and aureolin
with early evening clouds.

Everything in the garden
has reached the height of its verdure
and the day wilts.
The young greens are dulled to sage.
The chimney is the old blood
of hand-made brick
above azurite doors.
Each stone has its own potion of umber and gold.

The wattled hens and rusty bucket
are carmine by the pump.
Lime bright stones frame the ashy soil
where a woman bends
to the vegetation of the beds.

She pokes and pulls; he brushes and strokes.
Each sets this day into another;
into the half-life of minerals,
wood dust and dividing seed.

Soon the milked cows will low,
lumbering to the meadow
as they always have,
and the pigeons will stop clawing
the roof tiles and settle to roost.

The moon will fade in cloud
then brighten in its night
of indigo.
And the painter will have to go
and take this day into his mind's eye –
into another place – another sky.

Snowfall

This winter was cold, colder than
I remember winters being.
The snow fell softly
as down shaken lightly
from the blanket of sky, fleeing
its warm captivity. The span

of sky seemed smaller, tangible,
as if the cold solidified
invisible atoms of sky,
magnifying for the lazy eye
a hidden world now dignified
in velvety lace. Small miracles

showing the presence of unseen
laws beyond our constrained belief;
fragile pieces of divine space
fall, unstoppable as grace,
and seem to give the world relief
with a covering so soft and clean.

Constellation
For Michael

I am ten or twelve in a canoe on a Canadian lake.
It is night. Below me, a few metres of liquid blackness,
with its water spiders and snakes, its sharp schist islands,
above me the endless depth of space,
with its own archipelagos.

Each day we stayed on that island
I filled a bucket with lake water
and ladled it into cups with a battered tin dipper.
So I only recognised one place on that new sky map,
the Big Dipper, made from seven stars of Ursa Major.

I imagined it was full of nothingness,
scooped from the void,
carefully balanced in a strong and steady hand.
But since then I've seen it rotate and stand on end,
spilling darkness in a precise and careless arc,
reflecting this earth's tilt and spin.

Apparently from England
it looks like a plough.
These stars would coalesce and disperse
from any universal perspective,
but for you they will always furrow
the galaxies where star seeds grow.

For me it marks my place.
I am the part of the universe
from which it is a dipper
overflowing with space.

Three Fires – Solstice Song

Bone Fire

Bring clean bones
that once moved
that once grew
that even flew
make the fire new
and pile them on
then all will be pure and strong

And when it has been sung
when night fires are cold and done
gather the misty ash
take it to the summer fields
and fling it wide
sowing the seeds of death
and life

Wake Fire

Is there anything
more lovely than a tree in leaf –
its heart so soft and white?
But we will have it cut and dried
and take it to the pyre
for this fire
must be fierce and merry

Watch out for its beauty –
it makes you weep
with smoke and pain
for all that is gone
and comes again

St John's Fire

Prepare
for the waning of the year
now begun
the light reducing
to a singularity
when the head is struck from the day
the point when we say
look – a horizon
between the heavens and the earth

Such is our human sight –
the planets and suns
point to the now
when we believe
we can make our own stars –
like three lamps
guttering
in a desert night

The lighting of these three fires to celebrate midsummer is recorded at Lilleshall Abbey in the 15th century. St John's Fire honoured John the Baptist whose saint's day falls within the same week.

Autumn Findings

Swallow, swift and goose are gone,
but the bare tree in the garden is hung
with little birds plumped with song.

A giant wind panics crowds of leaves
and blows dandelion clocks of oak.
They flee, these famished evacuees.

The hungry flock alights as one,
then bolts in starling smoke.
But greedy bird's berry hangs down like a tongue.

Casting a shadow in low, fleeting sun,
the other I sense at my shoulder walks on,
ahead, into what is yet undone.

(ii)

The Other Land

Red Stag

I crawl into the beamed hall of his chest,
cover myself in skin and fur and creep
to sleep in the stretch of the skull.

While shoulders hunch and narrow
into legs and cloven points,
blood gathers from watery pools,
to its previous course. Muscle
binds to bone and then – eyes open.
My new body rises from its resting place.

I shake my heavy head of winter branches
and taste the air with bared teeth.
The wound on my haunch grows hair,
frosted stiff brown-grey.
Breath clouds soften throat and lips.
Hooves test the rocky slope.

Clearing the stings, I fly, and bracken blurs.
I am Herne the Hunter and his quarry.
I know the smell only and the speed.
The past is a dream and before me lies
the incline of earth, the thinning canopy,
flowing into field and shielding hedge.

I know the sound and the strange,
hard ground, but no longer what it means.
Arrows of light cross the scent trail – and I am hit.
Twenty paces of shattered bone till
I lie down here – a flood of blood in my belly –
torn haunch, from which a buzzard rises.

The Other Land

I feel it in the silence that follows a song
and the trap-gaps of coppiced trees
under bridges in the skin-pricking breeze

at the edge of places we don't belong.
It is found in the shadow of a hood
and the parted lids of a sleeping eye

even the twist of a rope that won't tie
or the path that unwinds in a wood.
It gathers its strength on a threshold

it unfolds in the hinge of the door
is crouching under a dusty floor
where old shoes keep its border patrolled.

It hides, like teeth behind a kiss.
Children understand the places in between.
They know what cracks mean:
any stone could fall to the abyss.

Creation Myth

Before time was measured and marked,
in the great black between the stars,
great beings lived, one of each kind.

Swift as a comet, Serpent curled and uncurled
through the void; always hungry, always in motion,
searching for something to fill his emptiness.

Timid Frog and Fish fled at his approach,
hiding in the same drift of a small galaxy.
After aeons, they gave in to their desires.

Their egg was full of water and mud.
The outer membrane stretched
as hordes of their offspring formed inside.

But when Serpent whipped past, he dislocated his jaws
and swallowed the giant egg whole. Already bigger
than anything he had eaten before, it continued to grow.

The Serpent's iridescent scales began to creak.
The egg was so delicious that he would not disgorge it,
in spite of the pain as he distended.

Soon he looked like an egg himself;
one that shone in the starlight, and moved in the depths.
His scales heaved up, like waves on a rough sea.

His seeping eyes erupted with fiery blood.
Water and Fire mingled, simmering together
body fluid, breath bubbles, bones and ash.

This alchemy formed a water jewel;
a blue-blazoned orb hanging on the neck of night,
spinning with the avaricious Serpent's struggle,
sometimes sheathed in rainbow,
sometimes wreathed in smoke.

White Horse

I can see you on a summer night
shaking out your mane
from the turf
skittish on the slope
never slowing toward the fall
where you will slake your thirst
in black water

afterwards you might walk the rise
to Dragon Hill and cast your eyes
over this England
the smooth roads of its towns
the shredded plastic of its verges
the flattened carcasses

and turn away

ascend the old Ridgeway
drought-marked
chalk-dry
kept by the edge
of polished bronze

going east to Wayland's forge
the cavelight barrow
where your nose stretches
for the scent of the old gods
firesmoke and slag
hammer and tongs

then newly shod
to canter the boundary west
ears pricked to Kingstone Coombes
and the gallops east
to Ram's Hill
declaring all is yours
to Idlebush

land claimed under your hooves
falls like water
down the crumbling hills
fresh earth and scree
the moon on your whiteness
the dark of years streaming
from your mane

Magpie Song

From one alone my power has grown –
a sevenfold mystery, unnamed and unknown

A treasure of two faces, black and white
acquisitive, hard as the edge of a knife

When backs are turned or eyes mid-blink
I'll take the foil or coin under wing

It's my street-boy smarts that no one likes –
the vicious gangs and roadside fights

No girl will catch me singing, or bake me
but cut me in half and I'm just more than three

I'm free lunch happy and dressed for dinner –
a blue flash suit for this entrepreneur

I'm worthy of respect and even fear
Don't agree? You'll shed a tear

If you hope to find . . .

The white hart behind the white well.
Glance aside, not for lance, do not spell
old enchantments. Let them sleep.
'Gently dip, but not too deep.'

The light that water casts on leaves,
the lips bent low to drink, the sacred dell.
Beyond the hedge of mist and tangled trees,
the white hart behind the white well.

Watched from some unhappy land
where many hear but do not tell,
old tales gasp, springs turn to sand.
Glance aside, not for lance, do not spell

out your lonely needs on these stones,
conjuring a new hero in his keep,
or a King riddled by his throne's
old enchantments. Let them sleep.

But go along the branching road
and find the fields, the hart's high leap.
And when you find your spirit's spring,
'Gently dip, but not too deep.'

A Glosa based on 'Usk' Landscapes – TS Eliot

Reindeer Hunt
The caves at Isturitz – Southern France

Nostrils flaring with an unease borne on the air,
the buck stands in front of its herd.
It will be rendered on the stone in red lines.
The curves of the cave will be its haunches,
the striations, its tendons.

A man lies on the part-frozen ground.
He watches the twitch of skin
across bellies taut with young.
He knows how the entrails will spill,
how the flint will part muscle from bone.

Thin tufts of grass are lined with frost,
and the deer stand out against the snow-bearing sky.
He already feels the grit of the iron oxide
on his fingers, tracing the line of the back
up the bristled neck to the antler's point.

Drawing back his spear thrower,
the hunter rises and shoots.
He hears the shaft strike and stay.
Hooves beat, hearts drum
and the herd is blown like smoke.

After twenty paces the buck's legs collapse.
It is on its knees, head back.
In its clouds of breath, droplets of blood
hang suspended.
This will be rendered in red pigment
shot through a reed from the painter's mouth
onto limestone air.

The hunter comes with his flint knife,
but the image is complete.
The painter's mind is empty.
With his hammer he will strike the curtain of stone.
He will live; the deer will live.

Virgin and Child

St Luke drawing the Virgin
by Rogier Van der Weyden, circa 1435

She sits upright in an open casement,
her back turned to the imperial battlements
embanking an azure river.

She wears a rich brocade of swirling flowers
and her face is a tender arc of brow, eye, lip.
With one hand she holds him,
with the other she offers her breast.

But he is a strange baby – naked, made of angles;
his fingers and toes are rigid in their flesh and skin.
There are creases around his eyes, almost from laughter,
or as if a great thing once gathered
had then been unfolded.

She brushes her nipple on his cheek,
waiting for him to turn and suck,
but he just looks at her and smiles.

This child, unconcerned by cold or hunger,
he will become the one who said:

'Is not life more important than food
and the body more important than clothes?'[1]

---

[1] Matthew 6:25

Infante Felipe Próspero 1659
Diego Velázquez

Notice his eyes first. He is looking at you,
wondering if you pose a threat.
His dog is no protection, lying, as it does,
on velvet like a discarded glove.
His amulets may draw your gaze next.
They hang on golden chains,
and his fingers, white as bone,
play with an incense ball.

Encased in cloth and kept inside,
away from hot light and cold wind,
he is pressed and pinned and prayed for.
Fingered by countless Asturian seamstresses,
who stitched and sneezed and coughed,
fed tidbits from the kitchens where
chefs spat and scullions wiped their noses;
he has no defence.

Behind him blackness gapes,
hiding the throne on which he will never sit.
Even without the sun, a palace has many shadows,
but this boy, already a ghost,
casts none but this.

The Mother Speaks

The marsh meets the sea, its master.
Banks are broken and the fresh blood
of frogs and snakes is stopped with salt.
Waves snatch chunks of earth to chew,
and all meat moves on muffled feet.
Muttering mead-soaked men who
gladly condemned our kind to Cain,
fearing the fiery ferment of our mere,
resolved to dig a drain and dry it.

So I must send my son, my boy,
armed and toothed with dread,
a hothead, always hungry,
to hunt for me in Hrothgar's hall.
My incantations have thickened his hide.
Rocks are no harder, oxen no stronger.
Let them hew; he will meet no harm.

Come son, wash well in the water,
with luck it will cover your smell.
Be stealthy and slip inside
the circle of staves where smoke rises,
and the tall posts of the traitor's hall.
Hinges will bend in your heavy hand,
so don't wake the dogs at the door.
Creep through the sleeping thanes and
slake your thirst at a throbbing throat.

Bring a young boy back and I'll blow
the keen of his death through my teeth.
But lead not the living to our lair,
Grendel. Stop their groans and grief
in your mighty grip and meet me here below.

(iii)

Where it may lead

Where it may lead

By streams of water, under sprung trees
they take off shoes to play –
cautious at first, testing tiptoe,
one footed.

Squatting on the deer-printed bank,
picking the fronds of bracken,
unfurled from baby fists,
they scatter them
and green frost patterns dimple the pool.

Their hopeful boats are ill equipped
for epic journeys.
Rudderless, they swing in an eddy,
almost submit to the depths,
drift into the dead realm
of an overhang and are caught.

Knee-deep rescuers free them
with long forked sticks
and steer the green skiffs
toward the breathless drop.
Some sink into grasping silt,
but, years on, emerge
with a family resemblance of fern or ash.

Others float on – join the slow glacier flow
of foam and willow
down the wide brown river,
watched by gyroscopes of butterflies,
waterboatmen and the rifle sight
of the heron.

Fishing

Shallow, lapping water pulls and warps the shadow
of a boy, braced before the morning with a rod.
His toes grip the silver weathered boards of the dock.
The lake is quiet, except for the creak of rope
and the virgin drop of the weighted hook when he casts.

Soon the cry comes – *Caught one!* On a hair's width,
the bent rod reels it in: a middling fish, fighting the air.
The boy is smiling, saying – *Hold still!*
Running his wetted hand down the sharp fin pricks,
he holds it up, face to face. The fish pants, staring.

The barb has pierced the pale cartilage around the eye
and cannot be unhooked. He puts it in the bucket –
for a breather – where it flick-flacks, tangling the line.
Bigger hands are called for, while the boy pleads –
Can't you see we're trying to help you?

The hook must come out the way it went in.
The open mouth of desire disgorges the bait
of temptation. Quickly slipped back in the bucket,
the fish fans its gills, and a small puff of blood disperses.
On his knees, the boy watches – saying nothing.

Quarried

Two sons – two dogs – a heavy pack,
skirting the edge of the old quarry
among the cowslips and sun.
And on the slope riddled with thorn,
my younger son met a fox cub in a thicket,
and heard its mother's gruff call –
Home.

The foxes went to ground,
and we, raising limestone dust,
followed the crumbling path down.
Above us rose the man-made cliffs,
intermittent with guano
and raven chicks.

Below our feet, a debt and accumulation:
tender stem turned stone, ammonitic forms
and the calcified sponges of the sea.
Still so much left,
and so much gone.

Let's stay here all day –
my older son said,
staring at the rubble all around.
Yes, all day – I said
and opened the pack, thinking:

what fossils were hewn
from me on the day of your birth
and all the days since?
And see what I have in return –
your mind an un-scaled cliff,
and the heart within, beating sound.

I am filled up –
full of cubs, cracked eggs,
downy feathers and flower stems –
the excreta of feeding and being fed.

And all the exquisite things that grow from the dead.

A Girl at Plage d'Erromardie

She is two years old –
no more –
and perhaps it's her first time
by the vast Atlantic
Running forward – anchored only by a mother's hand
she reaches out – points – fingers splayed
to tame the coming waves –
and they diminish at her command

Under a hat that won't stay
she suddenly buckles
wants to sit or crawl or lie –
and feel the sliding silver on her skin – the yielding sand
Hopping – thwarted –
she strains towards the water's indrawn breath
past foaming fingers
crawling in-land

The waves push – then
abruptly let go in their ancient endless game
This is for her singular delight
and mine. The ocean offers many sensations akin
to the fearless immersion of love –
loss of self –
and the feeling of being tossed
and held

Waters

The sac breaks suddenly, the flow begins.
I don't like to think of it, trapped inside,
a specimen without formaldehyde.

I wonder when it will evolve
and stop that flailing and flipping,
the water breathing. Inside my eyes
I've seen the gills and flaps of skin.

Contractions are waves from the deep ocean,
the swell of a gale – insistent, involuntary.
Pushes are white-capped breakers that carry
it to the messy shore of its mother's hands.

Wrapped in a rough towel, just a curl of wet hair,
he rails at the uncertainty of milk and air.

(iv)

Chameleon

Leverets

Huddled in a form, midfield,
their only protection from hawk and fox
is immobility and earth-brown fur.
Wide eyes can see the approach
of their doe or death equally well.

They are too small yet to learn
how to dodge and run;
how to make their hearts pump
power into legs, stretched
to launch the arrow of precarious life.

The hare bursts from the grass, runs,
switchback, tangling her scent trail.
The form is not a nest;
she suckles them sitting up.
Ear tips twitch. Nose dilates.

It may be a distant buzzard's call;
the stink of a vixen in the wind.
The leverets are still – perhaps they sleep,
briefly reassured and full.
She will go now, before they wake,
running before the talon, tooth and wheel.

Spring Lamb

They lie in the fields
abandoned to a death-like sleep,
like white washing fallen from the line.
Pick one up – it's just bones
covered in a crochet of silky wool,
and folds of skin waiting
to be swelled by milk and grass.

He waits for the bleat of his worn-out mother,
limping, chewing, half asleep.
She lets out a long stream of steam and urine;
her call a deep bass bellow,
and his long tongue cries – startling, loud.
His legs kick, so you let him go,
and he finds her with his hard forehead,
drinking like a jack hammer.

Soon he will sleep in a patch of bright grass,
his wool and belly will grow,
his folded ears will prick at strangers.
You will never catch him again –
but always remember the feel of his fleece –
that supple shroud.

Sleeping Dogs

Anywhere, abandoned
on floor or gravel,
or threadbare rug,
in sun, in shadow,
overwhelmed by need,
like babies
making their own blanket
of warm breath.

Their paws canter
to the muffled woof
at retreating enemies.
A chase on the retina
of the mind played out,
the muscles' work
in miniature.

We smile, are tempted
to touch and wake,
but let them lie.
Let them snatch
a faster, fiercer life.
Let them dream
the wolf inside.

Chameleon

He stayed with us for just three days,
but still we gave a name to him
for fun, and spoke to him about his eyes,
his toes and, most of all, his skin.

We played with him, not he with us.
We said he was too serious.
We laughed at his cautious, cartoon walk.
He frowned in concentration.

Even when we let him go, we smiled
at his escape, so slow and measured.
He will be happier in that thorny tree,
where everything, big or small, is as serious as he.

Words of the Naturalist
from Darwin's Commonplace Book – Galapagos

Disgusting lizards, like imps of darkness, crawl,
careless and clumsy, over the black, porous rocks;
an infernal habitat.

Insignificant, ugly flowers spring from this land.
They would better suit an arctic country,
not a tropical one.

Little finches, strangers to man, hop about in the bushes,
unwary of the stones we throw at them.
Mr King killed one with his hat.

Here are marvels! The tortoises think us innocent.
I pushed a large hawk off a branch
with the end of my gun.

What wonders there are, under this sun.

Redbreast

He pricked my conscience
in winter weather, with his cocked
black ice eye aimed at me –
ticking like a lookout
waiting for the drop –
chest swollen with downy air –
hunger-thin legs of sinew
taloned-strong.

I once heard his voice in a small room.
He perched on a teacup
by a window open to the Spring,
and his notes were melting ice,
coloured glass, beaten gold.

Go-between,
hopping on the cold dead days,
almost tamed,
landing on graves for worms,
here is seed for your breast,
your eyes,
your song.

(v)

Stained Glass Sequence

Poems inspired by the work of the artist
Margaret Agnes Rope

This Glass

This glass holds light
as cloud captures rain –
turning it into flowers
or wings – buses, boats
and brindled things –
the world's embrace.
See here a verdant place
of trees and pools
of quiet pain –
and memories of
a loved one's face

St Francis and the Birds

Poorly clothed in patches –
lower than the angels
with their showy silky wings –
he walked through the wide-mouthed world
with nothing

Befriended sun, moon
and wolf –
every creature of the Lord –
and understood the colour of their songs
from soaring blue to blood

So Francis – unfledged and slow –
spoke to birds with words – not seed
or crumb –
and felt the breath of wingbeats –
feathers folding in the sun

He counselled them to sing their praise –
for weight of air that holds the wing
for sticks and straw within
the nest – and nestlings
fat with flies

For wild flowers and wild bells
pliant earth and flailing worm
for nodding fern – and harvest grain
that falls to ground
and dies

Goblin Market
After the poem by Christina Rossetti

Gloaming brought the goblins out –
cat-face, rat-face, parrot, owl,
strange companions,
hind-legged, dressed
carefully in Sunday best.

But claws protrude
beneath their coats.
Their paws entwine
the lush grape vine,
gloating over
tender cherries
bursting berries
from some unnatural bush.

Obsequious and sly,
they cry –
Come buy, come buy!

But why?
Why believe their lie?

A brambling turns its gleaming eye.
A tit enticed by fragrant fruit
may alight and try –
or fly into the autumn wood,
as the girl's sister knew she should.

Why does she heed their wheedling cry?
Come buy!
The goblin craft enters the eye,
the ear, the mind –

and leaves a honeyed breath behind.
It stops the tongue –
like toadstool poison.

She will suck,
swallow, desire
and find that juice consuming fire.
Drink and eat –
so sweet, so sweet.

Come buy!
Come buy!

The Servant Speaks
Judith and the Head of Holofernes

Leaving the royal tent
and its dripping bed
where, like any sheep or goat,
she cut his throat and went on
cutting through his spine
to claim his head.

A lioness of Judah,
she stalked her prey,
did not say what she planned,
just called me in
to hold him down.
Now, she has wiped the sword
and left without a word,

her eyes fixed upon the hour
we reach our desert town,
and she presents her trophy
to the sighing elders
for their psalms of praise.
This blood from his neck has power
to save, like any paschal lamb.

Anointed and adorned,
she fears only God –
not armies, hardened by blood.
She will not look back
on her deed with alarm,
or the general's seeping, severed head
wet and heavy in my arms.

I tried to cover it with a sheet
but his mouth still seemed
to breathe in the scent of myrrh,
and out the smell of his defeat.
Wine and beauty made him weak
and now his lips hang loose
and he is silent
in the early morning air.

Soon there will be birds
and the guards will wake.
But Judith, of the shining hair,
pads out of camp
in starlit sandals
and garlands of beads
like meadow flowers,
leaving Assyrian men to comprehend
a woman was the end
of this tyrant's hours.

The Prodigal Self

I have known this self
within
who goes with feather flying
whistling in the wind
over-confident
wasting time
calling for more wine
stuffing her face
then losing at dice
unable to wait
That wandering self
who never knew
the value of what she had
who let it go
and got nothing
who was ungrateful
fell in with bad company
who embarrassed me
with her smell

And I have stood in the doorway
rigid with anger
at supposed repentance
and I have cried 'No' –
she must not share
the warmth or clothes
or steaming treats –
is undeserving
must leave in rags
go back to the pigs
the crow-cold heath

But compassion,
like a half-forgotten
dog at my heel,
creeps near
and leans its soft head
against my knee
glad to be home
happy with the barest bone
of unity thrown
on the floor –
and lies at my feet
in peace

St Winefride / *Gwenffrewi*

Scar across her neck –
cord across her waist –
band across her head –
this Winefride is sewn
together from
the pieces of a life –
cut, grafted
re-grown.

The staff of her authority
is sword-sharp –
so at its point
there flows
this water
from the wounded earth
to Gwytherin –
a place of hills
and depths.

A giver of health
in foxgloves
and the rowan's blood,
that feeds the birds.

Lifted free
from the orders of men,
like that water
which goes
wherever
it will,

like seeds
that can believe
in light and air.

Stained Glass Sequence

The six preceding poems were written during a residency
in Shrewsbury Museum & Art Gallery as part of the
exhibition 'Heavenly Lights: The Stained Glass Art of
Margaret Agnes Rope' in 2016.
The poems are based on the following artworks:

Sketch for St Francis Window –   *St Mary and St Michael,*
                                               Llanarth

Goblin Market – a student piece for Birmingham Art School

Judith and the Head of Holofernes – a student piece for
                                        Birmingham Art School

Sketch for the St Winefride Window – Holywell

Sketch for The Prodigal Son Window – St Mary's, Lanark

Margaret Agnes Rope (1882 – 1953) was born in
Shrewsbury and became a stained glass artist of
extraordinary vision and skill. Her work was influenced
by the later Arts & Crafts Movement, but has a focus on
the details of contemporary daily life that is unique.
Another striking quality is the attention to detail in flora
and fauna, especially many species of birds and flowers.
It seems that Margaret Rope was particularly fond of
dogs, often depicting them providing comfort and
companionship.

Her windows grace churches around the world.

Information and images can be found on the following
websites:

https://margaretrope.wordpress.com
http://www.arthur.rope.clara.net